Hot Food
&Warm Memories

Hot Food
& Warm Memories

a COOKBOOK from

SNUG HOLLOW FARM
BED & BREAKFAST

Pam,
Eat more pancakes

Barbara Napier, Innkeeper

Heart to Heart ❤️ Publishing, Inc.
528 Mud Creek Road
Morgantown, KY 42261
270-526-5589
www.hearttoheartpublishinginc.com

5th Reprint 2015

Cover Art: Kim White
Photography: Kim White *(cover)*, Robin Victor Goetz/www.GoRVGP.com *(pg. 24)*,
Taste of the South Magazine *(pp. 30, 46, 48, 79, 80, 81, 107)*, Jeff Rogers *(pg. 112)*,
Collin Staley, Kentucky Bed & Breakfast Association, and Barbara Napier

Illustration on page 127: Laura McNeel

Book Design & Composition: Barbara Napier and Dale Walker

Library of Congress: 2012944623

Special thanks for contributions from:
Taste of the South, Arts Across Kentucky, Kentucky Monthly, Midwest Living®,
National Geographic Traveler, Beth Curlin-Weber, Sharon Thompson, and Rona Roberts.

Barbara Napier
Snug Hollow Farm Bed & Breakfast
790 McSwain Branch
Irvine, Kentucky 40336

606-723-4786
www.snughollow.com

Printed in United States of America

This book is dedicated to Etta:
my mom, my mentor and my hero...

...and to my family.

I love you so!

Foreword

I will never forget the April day I first saw the farm. I hiked into the hollow because the road was hardly passable. Redbuds, dogwoods and acres of spring wildflowers greeted me as I walked along McSwain Branch creek that winds its way down from the mountains and through the farm.

I was the curious newcomer to a place with an old soul. Love at first sight is truly the phrase to use and it holds me to this day, 32 years later.

Grace, luck and fate have all had their hands on my life. Over the years I have learned to farm and garden, raised my sons and built my dream house. In the midst of learning and living I have had my share of loss. I even lost my farm but got it back. This is a story that deserves a book of its own.

Snug Hollow Farm Bed & Breakfast came together in the year 2000 and it is a continuing saga of creativity, straight-line energy and finding my true vocation.

I look forward to having you visit Snug Hollow Farm to enjoy our food and leave with your own warm memories.

Barbara

Acknowledgments

Everything I know, love and respect about cooking began with my mother, Etta and my sisters, Brenda and Kim. These are women of cream pies, fried chicken, chocolate cakes, homemade rolls and cheesecakes. Their kitchens have been their workshops for years as meringues and pie crusts, custards and ganaches are whipped up in an instant and without much ado. As a child I can remember raising money for school projects by raffling off my mother's butterscotch pies. Family members can only wish they score Brenda's custard for Christmas. Kim, a bona fide chef, is my "cooking by phone instructor" as she gives me the latest culinary fads and detailed instructions. The fact that she lives in Boston, a center of culinary excellence, gives credence to her recipes, all but the newest craze in soup. Tomato water? Not in Kentucky.

To cook and serve food brings joy and energy to my life. Just like Snug Hollow Farm, this cookbook is the result of the labor of many friends and dear family. Thanks to those who often gather at Snug Hollow to enjoy my love of cooking by sharing meals and allowing me to practice and give back what they, so freely, have given over the years.

A special thanks to my friend, Dale Walker who said "I'll help" and meant it. Her time, expertise, patience and humor brought my dream together. Thanks to Kim White and Bob Dundon for the beautiful and artistic covers. Their generosity has been overwhelming.

I appreciate Brenda Terry and Rhonda Childers for their tireless editing and suggestions. My gratitude goes to Tom Boyd for his unwavering support, to Dale and Lizzi for trying the recipes, and Nancy and Ed Lempke's insistence that I buy a good camera and trust my artistic ability. It paid off. Thanks to Judy, C. G. and Vicky for being there always.

I would like to thank Don and Beth Cunningham and Roy and Rhonda Welch for coming to my rescue by keeping everything working. Thanks to my sons, Mike and Todd Childers, for our new ovens, refrigerators and all the groovy updates to the kitchens.

Of course credit goes to Maria, Amy, Beth, Brenda, Matewood, B.C., Conor, Carrie, and Regina for giving me their time and hard work...cooking, serving, laughing and making me the star. Their friendship and appreciation for my cooking is inspirational. Every meal is a production and we do it over and over, and thanks to them, we enjoy it more and more.

Last but not least, I must express my appreciation to the guests who sit at my table and eat, rave about the food, ask for recipes, write wonderful reviews in our guest book, and ask, "When will the cookbook be ready?" This cookbook is for you, enjoy!

Hello
from
Snug Hollow Farm

wabi: simple, humble by choice and in tune with nature
sabi: the beauty inherent in the weathered patina of age

<u>*Wabi sabi*</u> *is a Japanese term celebrating all the marks that time, weather and loving use leave behind. Their beauty is in the cracks, chips, dents and stains. Their beauty is in their history.*

Snug Hollow is wabi sabi in the purist sense. Snaking through a crevice in time, the road to Snug Hollow descends to a place that visitors have called "heaven," a place truly at the end of the road.

Guests say it feels like home and its charm inspires and comforts the soul. The farm is 3oo acres of unspoiled beauty with deer, indigenous birds, wild turkeys and the simplicity of country life both past and present. You hear the sound of silence here.

almost there ...

Bird-song may be our greatest treasure on the farm.

The sound of silence is accompanied by a chorus of birds making their little voices heard throughout the valley. Over sixty species have been identified here and we are always ready for more. My birder friends and experts, the Papaya Girls, say Snug Hollow has all the right qualities to make it a bird haven: the lay of the land with its meadows, forests, water and deep undergrowth welcome and protect all types of birds.

Days begin with the enchanting call of the whippoorwill in season. Hummingbirds, cedar waxwings, indigo buntings, summer and scarlet tanagers, bluebirds and more are constant summer dwellers.

Spring is the peak of bird chatter. "Just getting home," "only passing through," "this nest is a mess," or "get up!" Autumn days are filled with shrill calls of red tailed hawks or the idle chatter of crows. Woodpeckers, nuthatches and our state bird, the cardinal keep us company in the winter.

For entertainment, there is an abundance of wildlife, fields of wildflowers and trails for hiking. The night sky, with its million stars and Milky Way, along with the occasional meteor shower, is a special treat.

farmhouse living room

Guests are welcome to lend a hand in the vegetable and flower gardens or spend an afternoon in the hammock by the pond.

Seasons are spectacular and there's no better place to enjoy them than from the many porches.

When the sun sets, whippoorwills begin to sing, barred owls hoot from both sides

"porch sitting" extraordinaire

of the hollow and coyotes sing their eerie chorales. Deer are spotted easily and, though he hasn't been seen, a bear sometimes leaves a calling card.

The Cozy Cabin is a 140 year-old restored chestnut log cabin with a panoramic view of the farm and horses. Reflecting the beauty and history of Snug Hollow, the upstairs bedroom has handmade quilts and feather beds, just some of the many comforts thought lost to the modern world. The tin roof makes even a rainy vacation special.

The Cozy Cabin is your home in the mountains. It is nestled in the trees making it very private. In spring and summer there are lots of fans, shady windows and breezes. The fireplace is perfect on winter days. The covered, private back porch looks out upon the mountains and overlooks the garden. Guests are welcome to enjoy the farmhouse amenities as well.

The Snug Hollow Farmhouse is as organic and eclectic as its architectural design. One's first view of the house is a surprise. It's a rambling two story structure of logs, natural wood and glass, designed to blend into nature, with open vistas to bring the outside in with no boundaries. Through the many windows, the walnut tree and the old cemetery are part of the décor. Antiques and comfortable furniture set the scene for quiet, intimate relaxation.

The house offers southern comfort, with a beamed living room, dining room, sun room and library, where you'll find a good selection of books, board games and music for all ages. No television. The upstairs bedrooms are reminiscent of Grandma's house. Each room has its own fantastic view.

While time stands still but passes way too quickly, the peace and beauty of Snug Hollow will linger for days to come. This snug little "holler" may add a new dimension to your life.

our farmhouse

Cooking is My Passion . . .

...and even though I am an amateur, my time in the kitchen is a calling. Cooking is not a chore here but a daily meditation. The planning, preparation and sharing of vegetarian meals are joys for me and gifts to our guests. At Snug Hollow, the sunny kitchen is the engine room of the house. Bread is baked daily; soups simmer on the stove and the pies in the oven fill the house with a fragrant promise of what's to come. Hearty breakfasts, lunches and elegant dinners are lovingly prepared and make their way to the table...another memorable meal!

I'm not sure if I was born to cook, but I sure have a love of preparing food my way. Since becoming a vegetarian 32 years ago I have searched for creative ways to cook and prepare delicious meals. My preference is to serve up old favorites with as little alteration as possible. Stuffed green peppers, pot pies, bean soup, mashed potatoes, macaroni and cheese or even a good cheesy pizza are my favorites.

Since a vegetarian diet may be confusing to some, this is a "what to cook" book as much as a recipe book. I have included ideas with familiar foods served in perhaps new and imaginative ways. I am flattered when guests ask for a recipe and I expect them to make it their own by adding or subtracting ingredients.

Having the right ingredient is important to Snug Hollow meals and we have a well-worn path from our garden to the kitchen door. When it comes to unconventional cooking, such as vegetarian, we must depend on our own "good taste." I mean this literally. By tasting, using herbs, spices and creative additions, you can give your dish the delicious taste it deserves.

"Tucked away in the hills of Estill County, Kentucky is a hide-away where guests can leave behind their fast-paced lives and truly relax. Snug Hollow is where innkeeper Barbara Napier treats you like royalty.

She does amazing things with home-grown vegetables and fruit and berries that grow wild on the hillsides. Sharing her recipes is just another way Barbara shows her true Kentucky hospitality."

Sharon Thompson

Sharon Thompson, Lexington Herald-Leader food editor, signs her book, Flavors of Kentucky, *at Snug Hollow.*

Winter months call for planning ahead and I make it a point to keep our cupboards well stocked with a good supply of winter keepers such as sweet potatoes, winter squash, apples and onions. Sunny window sills are crammed with favorite culinary herbs. At times I buy from local community growers and sometimes a trade is involved. That is the country way. Our country eggs are the real deal.

As I share my thoughts on a vegetarian lifestyle, I invite you to step into my world at Snug Hollow and into the spacious farmhouse dining room with a view of 300 scenic acres and sit down to a hearty meal of culinary delights. Candle light, fresh flowers and good company add to the ambiance of an exquisite dining experience.

Breakfast

BREAD

Snug Hollow breakfasts are served up

just like the morning, fresh, healthy and full of promise. Stacks of oatmeal pancakes, savory breakfast polenta, crispy cornmeal waffles, gingered bananas, biscuits with gravy and smoked cheddar omelets are just a few of our morning surprises.

We serve a familiar breakfast in a pleasing and healthy way. Fresh fruit smoothies are a summer flashback for the old hippies and a new-found-treat to the newer generation. Winter months bring dried fruit compotes and aromatic cinnamon rolls. Whatever the menu, when the dinner bell rings, breakfast is a real "come-and-get-it" affair.

Snug Hollow Oatmeal Pancakes

1 cup thick rolled oats   2 T. brown sugar
1 cup all-purpose flour   2 large eggs
½ cup whole wheat flour   2 cups buttermilk
2 ½ t. baking powder   5 T. butter, melted
pinch of salt

In a large mixing bowl, add all dry ingredients. Mix well. In another bowl, beat the eggs and stir in buttermilk and butter. Combine wet and dry ingredients and stir well. Let mixture rest while you heat the griddle. Add a little more milk to the batter if too dry. Use cooking spray to prevent sticking. Pour out batter by the

½ cup. Pancakes are generally ready to turn when they first begin to bubble and stiffen on top. For light, fluffy pancakes, refrain from flipping more than once. Add blueberries after pouring onto griddle if you'd like. Heat maple syrup and garnish with gingered bananas. Serves 3 hungry people.

Gingered Bananas

We serve this golden goody on our oatmeal pancakes and French toast. Homegrown peaches may be substituted.

1 banana, sliced
1 T. freshly grated ginger
2 T. butter
water (if needed)

Melt butter in a small skillet over low heat. Add ginger and bananas. Add a teaspoon or two of water to skillet to prevent burning, if necessary. Stir and let simmer 1 minute and spoon onto pancakes. This is enough bananas for 1 pancake recipe.

Biscuits

The secret to great, fluffy biscuits is to handle them as little as possible. Remember, for tall biscuits, have your dough thick. This recipe makes 12 plump biscuits.

2¼ cups heavy whipping cream
2 cups self-rising flour

Preheat oven to 450°

Pour heavy whipping cream in a medium mixing bowl and add flour gradually. Stir together until wet and dry ingredients are blended well. May need to adjust cream or flour. Turn biscuit dough onto floured board. Using whole wheat flour, gently pat dough to about 1-inch thickness.

Using a biscuit cutter dipped in whole wheat flour, cut out biscuits and place on baking sheet not touching. If you don't have a biscuit cutter, you may use the open end of a juice glass.

Bake biscuits for 15-20 minutes, or until lightly browned. We pass the warm sorghum or homemade jam.

Gravy

In medium skillet, make roux by mixing:

3 T. melted butter
2 T. flour
2 T. heaping nutritional yeast
2 T. Tamari sauce
black pepper
salt
sage and thyme to taste
2 cups milk

Brown the flour and yeast in melted butter. Stirring constantly, add Tamari, then milk, and season to taste. Cook until thick. You may need to add more milk before you serve.

We serve gravy over hot biscuits with sliced fresh tomatoes.

cherry coffee cake

Cherry or Blackberry Coffee Cake

We often use our own homemade jams for these, but sometimes our guests send us a sample of their favorite homemade delights. Whichever, they are delicious. Makes 2 cakes and freezes well.

Cake
2 T. active dry yeast
¼ cup warm water
¾ cup butter
¼ cup sugar
2 T. brown sugar
4 eggs (reserve 1 egg white)
4 cups all purpose flour
¾ cup heavy cream
1 t. water

Filling
1 cup cherry or blackberry preserves
½ cup chopped pecans
½ cups sugar or honey
½ cup soft butter

Dissolve yeast in water. Cream together butter, sugars and salt in a mixer bowl. Add 3 eggs + 1 yolk, one a time, beating well after each egg. Stir in flour alternately with yeast and cream. Mix but do not beat. Setting aside one cup of dough, spread the remainder in 2 greased 9 x 9 x 2 inch baking pans. (A floured spoon will help smooth the dough.)

To make filling, combine preserves, butter, pecans and sugar or honey. Mix well. Spread filling over dough in each pan.

For a pretty lattice top, blend flour into remaining dough and roll to a 9 inch square on a floured surface. Cut into 16 strips and arrange strips in lattice pattern over filling in each pan. Beat together egg white and water and brush over strips of dough. Cover pans and let rise in warm place until doubled or about 30 minutes. Bake at 375° for 15-20 minutes until lightly browned.

Crispy Oatmeal & Cornmeal Waffles

Amy's homeground cornmeal is the secret to this crispy special breakfast.

½ cup unbleached flour   1 cup milk +1 T.

½ cup cornmeal   6 T. melted butter

4 t. baking powder   2 large eggs, beaten

3 T. brown sugar   1 cup heavy cream

¼ t. salt   1¼ cups thick rolled oats

We use thick oats from a health food store.

Heat waffle iron on medium-high and oil generously. Mix together dry ingredients. Stir in eggs, cream, butter and milk. Let stand 2 minutes and bake in hot waffle iron on medium. Keep an eye on them, these waffles crisp up quickly. We serve them with real maple syrup and yogurt with fruit.

Cooking Tips

Cooking and baking are so different. Cooking allows me to use my preference as to how much of an ingredient to use but baking is an exact science. Like many cooks, I may add a pinch or a handful of ingredients in a recipe. The dilemma is the exact amount. If I were to have a measurement table it would look like this.

Small amount = little bit
Some = a few
Generous amount = a lot

Hope this doesn't cause too much grief for anyone trying out a recipe, but it is the Snug Hollow way and I would guess is the rule in many kitchens.

"Secret ingredients" may not be the phrase I'm looking for, but when asked what gives our Kentuscan bean soup the meaty flavor that makes you want to drink it, I tell the story of my friendship with Tamari sauce and nutritional yeast. Just as bacon and eggs, salt and pepper and milk and honey go hand in hand, so do nutritional yeast and Tamari sauce in vegetarian cooking. A melding of the two creates a meaty, salty taste that enhances most any dish. To say I use them freely is an understatement...I wish I could purchase them by the 55 gallon drum. Both these ingredients may be found at your local health food store.

Nutritional yeast is a yellow, non-rising yeast powder with a nutty taste. High in protein, it is also a source of B vitamins. Try it sprinkled on popcorn, yum.

Tamari sauce is soy sauce made of soy beans. It has a deep meaty, salty taste. Tamari sauce and nutritional yeast, mixed with generous amounts of olive oil or butter, make a perfect addition to a roux for gravies, sauces or soups.

Fruit Smoothies

Be creative with your fruit. Mix whatever you have and you'll find it delicious and so colorful. We freeze bananas that are getting soft and use them in breakfast smoothies.

⅓ cup plain yogurt
⅓ cup orange or any juice.
fresh or frozen fruit:
  bananas, strawberries, blackberries,
  blueberries and peaches

We often freeze some of our fruit the night before. Fill the blender ¾ full with fruit, add yogurt and juice. You may add a couple of ice cubes. Blend until smooth and frothy. Pour into frosted glasses. Serve immediately.

French Toast

French toast is a delicious way to use leftover Snug Hollow Rosemary Bread.

---

bread, thickly sliced
butter
1 egg, beaten
⅓ cup milk
apple butter
syrup

Dip bread slices in egg and milk mixture and spread with apple butter on one side.

On heated griddle or skillet, melt small amount of butter and add bread slices. Fry until browned and crisp. Turn over and repeat. Pour small amount of real maple syrup over toast and let warm on griddle.

*Conor loves
Nana's French toast*

"Dear Barbara,

We came to trace our Kentucky ancestors but we leave with so much more than we ever expected. We'll never forget the fabulous food, fantastic company and gracious hostess. We are so fortunate to have found Snug Hollow and all its magic. You are truly a sparkling gem in these hills. Keep shining- and like the others before us- we can't wait to return!"

Cindy, Melanie & Bobbie

Cranberry Sweet Dough

This is a scrumptious winter morning treat served warm with just a smidgen of fresh cream. It is also a beautiful winter holiday dessert.

¾ cup butter, softened
1¾ cups fresh cranberries
½ cup coarsely chopped pecans
⅓ cup sugar
½ cup brown sugar

1 egg
½ cup all purpose flour
⅛ t. ground cloves
⅛ t. salt

Preheat oven to 325°. Coat sides and bottom of 8" baking dish with oil or butter.

Spread cranberries evenly over bottom of dish. Sprinkle on pecans, sugar and cloves.

Melt butter in saucepan over medium heat and set aside. In a bowl, combine egg and brown sugar. Beat with electric mixer until pale and thick. On slow speed, mix in flour and add salt and butter. Mix well and pour over cranberries in baking dish. You may need to smooth it with a spoon to get a good cover. Bake until golden about 30 minutes or until center tests done. Remove from oven, run knife around sides and cool. Turn onto serving plate.

Cranberries

We serve fresh cranberries with lots of our meals. They compliment such dishes as our Kentuscan bean soup, or stir-fried greens and pasta. Cranberries are really delicious with a hot macaroni and cheese dish.

1 bag fresh cranberries
sugar
whole cloves

Cook cranberries according to package directions. I add a few whole cloves before cooking.

Butter Jam Kuchen

This yeasty coffee cake is one of my favorites when we make it with apricot jam. We also use orange marmalade or our homemade apple butter. It has very little sugar for those who watch such things. These freeze well.

---

2 cups all purpose flour
3 T. dry yeast
½ cup milk
6 T. butter
1 egg
½ cup sugar
¼ salt
¾ cup warmed jam or preserves
(apricot is delicious)

Topping
½ cup flour
½ chopped pecans or walnuts
⅓ cup brown sugar
¼ cup butter
½ t. vanilla

Combine 1 cup of flour and yeast. Warm milk, sugar, butter and salt, stirring just until butter melts. Add to flour and yeast and add egg. Beat at low speed with mixer for about ½ minute and then 3 minutes at high speed. By hand, stir in enough remaining flour to make a soft dough.

Spread in two greased 8" pans and cover. Let rise about 30 minutes or until doubled. Using a large spoon, make depressions at intervals in the raised dough and fill them with warm jam or preserves.

To make topping: Combine flour, pecans or walnuts and brown sugar. Cut in butter and vanilla. Sprinkle half the topping over dough in each pan and bake at 350° for about 20-25 minutes.

Kentucky Fried Apples

Fried apples were served every Sunday morning at our house. Mom knew how to make our breakfast a special occasion. We do the same on the farm.

3 cups thickly sliced apples
(any apples except Red Delicious)
1 T. grated ginger root
butter
brown sugar

Melt enough butter to cover bottom of large skillet. Add grated ginger root and heat for a minute. Add sliced apples and sprinkle brown sugar on top (you may add a couple tablespoons of water to prevent burning and help cook down apples a bit). Cover and fry over medium heat for about 10 minutes.

At this point, take off lid and give the apples a stir. Apples are ready when they are soft and browned. This will make 3-4 servings.

Our dinner bell came from my Dad when I moved to the farm 32 years ago. He said, "You'll need this someday". He was right! We ring it before breakfast and dinner to bring our guests to the table.

Blackberry Shortcake

Our guests love to pick blackberries on the farm. If we are lucky they won't eat them all, and we can make blackberry shortcake for breakfast.

4 cups fresh or frozen berries
1 cup sugar
sprinkling of ground cloves
1 T. flour

Place all ingredients in a saucepan and slowly bring to a boil. Stir constantly until it boils. Reduce heat and cook, stirring constantly for about 3 minutes. Remove from heat and cool slightly.

We serve our berries over Snug Hollow biscuits with cream for breakfast or top it off with ice cream and freshly whipped cream for dinner desserts.

Gingered Peaches

4 cups sliced fresh peaches   1 big T. fresh ginger, shredded
¼ cup water   ½ cup brown sugar

Place all ingredients in a skillet and bring to a slow boil. Reduce heat and cook for about 1 minute, stirring constantly to prevent burning. Turn off heat and let cool slightly. Serve over ice cream.

Polenta Breakfast Fries

What is locally known in Kentucky as fried cornmeal mush, is known in culinary circles as polenta. We make our polenta with quick grits and water.

4 cups water	½ t. sage and thyme
salt	hot pepper flakes
1 T. Tamari sauce	1 T. nutritional yeast
2 cups grits	oil
6 T. butter	1 cup flour

Combine water, butter, Tamari, herbs, yeast, salt, and pepper flakes to taste in a heavy pot over medium-high heat. Bring to a boil, reduce heat and slowly stir in grits. Stir constantly until polenta pulls away from the sides of the pan and most of the liquid has been absorbed.

Transfer polenta to a 9x13 sheet pan lined with plastic wrap and spread to fit pan. Smooth top with spatula and refrigerate uncovered until chilled and set. Pour oil into heavy skillet and heat over medium heat until hot. Cut polenta into 1" sticks, coat with flour and fry until crisp, turning once. Drain on paper towels. Serve with eggs, pancakes or waffles.

Country Fried Potatoes

5 medium potatoes (we grow Yukon Gold or Red Cloud)	salt and pepper
	Tamari sauce
oil for frying	sage
nutritional yeast	thyme

Cut potatoes into ½-1 inch cubes. Heat the oil in a large skillet. Pour potatoes into hot oil. Sprinkle on nutritional yeast, Tamari, sage and thyme. Cover and fry, stirring occasionally to prevent burning. Remove cover when potatoes began to soften and continue to fry until potatoes are crisp. Drain. Add sea salt and freshly cracked pepper before serving - 4 servings.

Breakfast Tofu

1 block firm tofu   Tamari sauce
(not previously frozen) nutritional yeast
oil for frying

Squeeze and drain tofu block to remove as much water as possible. Let it drain on a paper towel for a few minutes. Slice tofu into thin ¼- ½ inch slices. Heat enough oil to barely cover bottom of skillet and add tofu. Sprinkle each slice liberally with Tamari and nutritional yeast. Fry on both sides until crispy. Drain on paper towel and serve.

Tofu and Tomato Sandwich

A "TLT" takes the place of a BLT at Snug Hollow. Crispy Tofu and fresh summer tomatoes from the garden on our toasted bread is GREAT! This is good anytime for lunch or a picnic.

Eggstraordinarily Scrumptious Scrambled Eggs

9 large country eggs, separated
splash of milk
cream cheese

Beat whites until frothy and yolks until blended. Pour together. Add 2 T. cream cheese and a splash of milk. Stir slightly and pour into hot oiled skillet and lower heat. Stir frequently until done. Serve immediately. Serves 4.

Tofu or bean curd is made by curdling the white "milk" of the crushed soybean. It may be prepared in various and delicious ways. The recipes listed here are all original and are very tasty. We don't serve our tofu dishes often at Snug Hollow, but when requested they are always a hit at the table. Tofu is an excellent source of protein, low in fat, carbohydrates and calories. It contains no cholesterol and is readily available in supermarkets or your local health food store. As an alternative to meat, this high source of vegetable protein is easily digested and an alternative for dairy-free cooking. Tofu may be used as is or after freezing. When frozen, tofu becomes chewy and absorbs any sauce that is added.

Fried Potatoes
and Smoked Cheddar Omelet

9-10 large country eggs	*½ t. sea salt*
splash of milk	*1 cup smoked cheddar, grated*
1 T. nutritional yeast	*½ t. pepper*
oil for frying	*sage and thyme*
2 T. Tamari sauce	*2 medium red potatoes, thinly sliced*

In a large skillet, pour in ½ cup oil and place on medium heat. When oil is hot, add potato slices. Sprinkle nutritional yeast and Tamari over frying potatoes and add salt, pepper, sage and thyme. Cover and fry until golden brown, stirring occasionally. Remove from heat. Place 10 large eggs into large mixing bowl. With a mixer, beat eggs on high until fluffy and add milk

Drain oil from the potato skillet, arrange potatoes to cover the bottom of the skillet and place on medium heat. Pour egg mixture over potatoes. As eggs start to thicken, use a spatula to move egg mixture around the pan for even cooking. Cover and cook over low heat until set, stirring or flipping when needed. Sprinkle smoked cheddar on eggs, lower heat and replace lid until cheese is melted. Cut into wedges and garnish with tomatoes and a basil leaf. Makes 5 servings.

pickin' after breakfast

"As I began to write, a fawn was leaping across the upper hillside, lost from his mama…and the horses were snoozing in the sun. Birds had provided a symphony wake up call this morning…As I stood last evening amazed at the night sky I wept. God's wonder and majesty are on full display here…and as evident in the loving care that Barbara has given in tending his land. Our honeymoon could not have started in a more relaxing way-time for just us, with no distractions, except the beauty and peace of Snug Hollow. Blessings!"

Dixie Taylor
Simpsonville, KY

Breakfast Fruit Tart

*Since this crust is very crumbly we use a pan with
a removable bottom for easier serving.*

½ cup plain yogurt
1 cup cream cheese
your choice of fruit
1 jar unsweetened apricot jam
1 short crust recipe

Press short crust into tart pan. Bake at 350° until lightly browned.
Cool and place on serving dish. Mix together, cream cheese and
yogurt and carefully spread on short crust. Slice fruit to cover filling.
You may use strawberries, bananas, grapes, blueberries, etc. Warm
unsweetened apricot jam and pour carefully to cover fruit. Cool and
serve with crème fraîche.

*"The intangibles are what
make this place rise above all
others, the sounds of horses, a
tin roof creaking in the sun
and the smell of fresh country
air. Blessing to you for all
you do for us, your visitors,
we can honestly say we don't
want to go home."*

Mike & Lynn

Crème Fraîche

1 cup buttermilk

2 T. sour cream

Stir together, cover and let
sit for 8 hours. Stir well and
refrigerate.

breakfast fruit tart

Welcome to my garden

*A garden is a valued asset in mountain culture
where we grow it, eat it, dry it, or can it.
That simple.*

My garden is a celebration of the "giving" spirit of Snug Hollow Farm. Long growing seasons, bountiful harvests and restful fallow times are true gifts of this land. What an inspiration to find myself on my knees in the soil, planting or weeding only to be interrupted by the long howl of a coyote, the shrill call of a swooping red tailed hawk, or a surprise rain storm. Moments like these bring a stillness to feel and listen to the world around me. Misty spring mornings, summer evenings and fall days call me to the garden to "enjoy an old friend."

My first gardening experience was Mom's garden and it was truly "her garden." We were allowed to enter but this was her world. My mother was an avid follower of Rodale's Organic Gardening and her garden was a showpiece in our rural town. Small and compact, it was chocked full of a variety of vegetables that supplied our family and neighbors with fresh food all summer.

After moving to the farm, I owned and operated a Farm Service Center. This experience and studying horticulture at a local university gave me some knowledge of soils, vegetable varieties and their hardiness in this area. Both whetted my appetite to get my hands dirty and to begin my own organic garden. Soon I did just that!

Mom had a special blender that she only used for the garden. She would remove any pests such as Japanese beetles, bean bugs or squash beetles, throw them into the blender with some peppers and water. This became a plant spray that was the most effective pest control I have ever witnessed. My dad always checked to see which blender we used for our milk shakes.

Through my years as chief gardener at Snug Hollow, the garden has played different roles in my life: friend, teacher, business partner, nourishment of mind, body, spirit, and more.

Gardening organically has been an adventure that has led me down many roads. In the beginning, new information came quickly and Mom's suggestions were inspiring, but in the end, I have found experience to be my best teacher. It's the overnight miracle of gardening that keeps me loving it so. The first turning of the beds, dropping the tiny seeds into the black, cavernous earth, hidden from life-sustaining sunlight, always tests my faith in Mother Nature.

The garden quickly became a business opportunity as my entrepreneurial spirit led me to start a CSA (Community Supported Agriculture). This time spent in my garden was the most creative of my life. Certifying the farm as organic, selecting and planting the crops and lavishing them with love and sweat equity paid off.

Community Supported Agriculture (CSA) is an agreement between the grower and the consumer. The consumer says, "We value our food, how it's grown and who grows it." The grower and the consumer take the growing risks together. Everyone is a winner, with good food, friendships and an understanding of where the food is grown.

summer bounty

The customers appeared and the garden soon became my center of community and a place of inspiration.

I called my business "Plot Luck," and from May until October I delivered baskets of vegetables every two weeks. The CSA and its newsletters were much appreciated by the "Plot Luckers" and many of them still spend quality time at the farm.

Years after closing the CSA, I still nurture the garden. It has taken its place, and rightly so, at the head of the table.

Over the years the garden has had many friends lending a hand and heart for its success. Meg, a born gardener, friend and capable intern spent her summers creating a most beautiful and bountiful landscape.

My friend, Tom, gave his all to some of our most productive and glorious gardens. Long days of spraying each plant tendril with "fish fertilizer" was his meditation, and we haven't had 12 foot sunflowers since.

gardener Meg

The garden has been my companion for over 30 years and has given me the opportunity to share my harvest and make new friends. Today as Snug Hollow Farm "feeds and cares for" its many guests, the garden continues to work its magic.

"A Girl Gardening Tip"

Digging was always a hard job until I discovered the "landscape" or "rose shovel." Sometimes it is called a diamond mouth shovel and it has a sharp rounded edge that will make a dent in any type of soil. The flat spades that so many gardeners recommend just don't work for me. You will either find these at a garden center or by special order.

Food Column for Earth Day

Nougat Magazine, April, 2008

My own environmental awakening is taking years, with lots of repeat taps on the snooze button. Barbara Napier, though, has been awake for decades. In honor of Earth Day (April 22), I want you to meet her.

Let's work backward. In 2007 Barbara's exquisite Snug Hollow Farm B&B became a recognized "Green Hotel". Honoring Barbara's achievements, three prestigious regional development groups jointly named her the small business "2007 Entrepreneur of the Year for Southeastern Kentucky."

The Summer 2007 issue of *Taste of the South* magazine features a nine-page full color spread on Snug Hollow, describing Barbara as "an artist in the truest sense of the word, a person whose imagination changes the way we see the world." Barbara says, "I consider Snug Hollow my canvas. I love to set scenes that catch people's eye and heart."

What a canvas: a 300 acre working organic farm, circled by gentle mountains, at the end of a gravel road in Estill County, 53 miles from my downtown Lexington home. Add water features – creeks and a small lake. Insert wildlife, wild flowers, a log cabin, a gracious new small inn built of salvaged materials.

Picture breezy porches, bright sunrooms, fireplaces, and tables dressed with brilliant organic food and flowers from the Snug Hollow gardens. In winter, cue utter, blissful quiet. The warmer season soundtracks feature bird-song, spring peepers, katydids, whippoorwills, cicadas, crickets. Honoring Barbara's artistry with these original materials, author Marybeth Bond included Snug Hollow in the 2007 edition of *50 Best Girlfriend Getaways in North America*, published by *National Geographic*.

When I first met Barbara several years ago I learned some of her dramatic life story. She launched a successful organic CSA (Community Supported Agriculture vegetable "subscription" program) in Estill County years before I heard of the concept.

Sometime earlier, she ran a feed store in Irvine with her husband. When they divorced, Barbara lost her business and farm. Barbara took a job away from the farm. With friends' help, she bought the farm back, built the three-story inn and launched her B&B on New Year's Eve in 2000.

Each of Barbara's eco-businesses has seemed ahead of its time in Kentucky, and yet each has succeeded. I asked Barbara what led her to launch her CSA before organic was cool, and her answer surprised me.

"Well, actually organic was cool -- just not in the national news. I had no trouble getting more customers than I could attend to. My 25 customers really looked forward to the vegetables and all of them loved my newsletters, too. After operating a Farm Service Center, selling feed, seed and fertilizer, I realized that organic would be so much easier, and it really seemed attractive after the chemical stuff."

Barbara's artistic imagination may have helped her succeed as an eco-friendly entrepreneur. Defying conventional views, Barbara envisioned people as eager to support earth-friendly ventures. I would have guessed we are too much in denial to care about supporting green businesses and lessening our negative impact on the earth. I would have been wrong.

Barbara's success comes from her prodigious joyous energy – in a past life she must have been a verb – and from capitalizing on our readiness to go green at the table, green at our hotels and retreats, green in our lives. At Snug Hollow, instead of longing to pull the covers over our head and leave it to someone else to save the earth, we visitors embrace a new possibility: maybe we can change how we relate to the earth and enjoy the change deeply.

Barbara makes eco-change taste, look, and feel good. Waking up to our responsibility for the earth just got a lot more appealing. Thank you, Barbara Napier!

Rona Roberts, *Nougat Magazine*, April, 2008
Rona hosts savoringkentucky.com

Soups

Kentuscan Bean Soup

This is a very brothy and fragrant soup, a Snug Hollow original.
You may serve it as an entrée with cheese grits, or as a soup course.

---

2 small cans of great northern beans, rinsed
½ stick butter
3 T. chopped fresh garlic
2 T. chopped fresh rosemary
1 T. rubbed sage
2 T. Tamari sauce
2-3 T. nutritional yeast
2 cups water
½ t. black pepper

In saucepan, melt butter over medium heat; add garlic, rosemary, sage and pepper. Cook slowly for a few minutes.

Add Tamari sauce and nutritional yeast and stir until mixed. Add water and great northern beans (rinsed well) or you may substitute with a can of pinto beans. Bring to slow boil and simmer for about 10 minutes and remove from heat. Warm before serving. Makes 4 large servings.

"There is music from the earth and here we found a symphony. Birdsong, the beauty of a mountain glade strewn with blue cohash, day walks, moonlit walks, peepers, barred owls and bullfrogs. You are so blessed. We are so blessed that you chose to share! Thank you Barbara, with love and spirit. "

The Papaya Girls
Frankfort, KY

Summer Melon Soup

On hot sultry summer evenings, we "chill out" by serving our melon soup at the beginning of our dinners. I prefer honeydew and cantaloupe.

½ *honeydew and* ½ *cantaloupe – your choice of melon*
1 lime

Slice, peel and remove seeds from melons. Puree each melon separately in food processor. Add a little honey to cantaloupe if necessary. Put melon puree in freezer until it begins to freeze. Serve in small frozen bowls, pouring soups simultaneously to swirl naturally in bowl. Squeeze on fresh lime juice or spoon on crème fraîche. Serves 4.

Hillary, our little "Jane Russell", is one of the co-founders of Snug Hollow and greets everyone with the enthusiasm of a Kentucky thunderstorm. She thinks everyone has come to see her, and lots of our guests have and don't even know it until they get here. Hillary always wins over even the most canine reluctant visitors and before long they are fast friends. Goodbyes are hard for her!

Split Pea Soup

Hot split pea soup and baked sweet potatoes make a hearty winter dinner.

---

1 lb. bag split peas
5–6 cups of water
3 T. butter
1 bay leaf
1 onion, chopped
3 stalks celery, chopped
2 cups thinly sliced carrots
1 thinly sliced potato
3 T. Tamari sauce
3 T. nutritional yeast
pinch of fresh rosemary and sage
salt and pepper
1 T. Liquid Smoke (optional)

In a saucepan, combine butter with onions, celery, bay leaf, Tamari and nutritional yeast. Sauté until soft. Add split peas, water, salt, pepper and bring to a boil. Skim off foam, cover and continue cooking on medium heat for about 30 minutes.

Add carrots and potatoes when other vegetables are almost tender. Continue to cook for about 20 minutes, then remove bay leaf. When ready to serve, pour ¾ of soup in blender and blend until smooth. Pour into remaining soup and add Liquid Smoke (optional). Stir and season to taste. Serves 8-10 people.

Tasty Vegetable Soup

Vegetable soup on the farm is a presentation of our best garden vegetables. We like it with lots of broth and served in huge bowls topped off with pesto.

---

2 potatoes, cubed

1 onion, peeled and chopped

2 stalks celery, sliced thin

3 large carrots, sliced thin

2 cloves fresh garlic, minced

Tamari sauce/nutritional yeast

1 small can red kidney beans, drained

1 cup small pasta – small bow tie or shells

16 oz. can tomatoes, puréed

2–3 cups water

1 T. dried oregano

1 cup frozen peas

1 cup chopped parsley

1 large can V8 juice

½ cup dried lentils

3 T. olive oil

fresh or frozen basil

In a large soup pot, heat oil and sauté onion, celery and garlic. Pour in V8 juice, water, tomatoes, kidney beans, carrots, parsley, lentils, potatoes, oregano and basil. Add salt, pepper, Tamari sauce and nutritional yeast to taste. You may add extra juice or water to make a brothy soup.

Cover and simmer until vegetables are barely cooked. Add frozen peas and small pasta, cover and let sit for 10 minutes. Soup may need a little more cooking, but do not cook until mushy! Warm soup before serving.

Drizzle pesto on top and serve with a fresh salad and a cheese soufflé. Don't forget the freshly baked bread, cornbread is best. Serves 10 people.

Some years our scarecrow becomes one of the family. This snowy day made her red scarf seem so appropriate. Just couldn't take her down!

Vegetarian Chili

I have made vegetarian chili for years and I'm always surprised as to how much of any ingredient I add. Here is an attempt at ingredient amounts, but I will leave it up to you as to how much to use.

---

1 cup each, chopped onions, celery, bell peppers
2 T. olive oil and butter
basil, oregano, whole cumin , chili powder – to taste
¼ cup of nutritional yeast
2 T. Tamari sauce
2 large cans chopped or stewed tomatoes
large can V8 juice
½ cup chopped sundried tomatoes
small can diced green chilies
1 large can kidney beans, rinsed, or cook your own
½ chopped dried chipotle pepper (if you don't like it hot, remove seeds)
½ cup dried lentils
water, salt and pepper
1 t. Liquid Smoke
pinch of cayenne pepper

In a large pot, sauté onions, celery, bell pepper in olive oil and butter. Add basil, oregano, cumin, chili powder, nutritional yeast and Tamari sauce.

Add tomatoes, V8 juice, sundried tomatoes, green chilies, kidney beans, chipotle pepper and lentils. Add salt, pepper and water to make broth. Cook over medium heat until thick and tasty.

Butternut Squash Soup

We serve this soup warm in the winter and slightly frozen in the summer. You may freeze any leftover squash and thaw to prepare soup. Butternut squash is a good keeper and we have lots on hand throughout the winter.

---

1 medium butternut squash
2 T. curry powder
whipping cream
cayenne pepper
water

Cut squash in half, wrap in foil and bake until soft. Remove from oven, dip out seeds. I do not peel the squash.

Place squash pieces in a blender, add small amount of water and enough whipping cream to make a dense soup. Blend well.

Add curry and pinch of cayenne.

Top hot soup with a swirl of warm molasses. For a summer treat, place in freezer just until icy and serve in frosty bowls. This will make 8-10 small servings.

Spicy Lentil Soup

We often serve this soup over brown rice for a more filling entreé. A dollop of chutney and a cucumber salad are tasty accompaniments.

2 T. olive oil
1 large onion, peeled and chopped
3 large carrots, sliced thin
3 stalks celery, chopped
1 bay leaf
1 quart canned tomatoes
3 cups water
2 cups lentils
salt and pepper
Tamari sauce
nutritional yeast to taste
1 T. curry powder
¼ t. ground ginger
a few whole cloves
¼ t. cinnamon
pinch cayenne pepper

don't forget the homemade bread

Heat the oil in a large soup pot. Sauté celery, onions and carrots. Pour tomatoes in food processor and blend well. Add to soup pot with water, lentils, Tamari sauce, nutritional yeast, salt and pepper. Simmer on low heat until soft. In a small pan, heat butter, bay leaf and spices until fragrant. Pour into soup mixture and simmer for 10 minutes. Serves 4-5.

Homemade Tomato Soup

Everybody's favorite. This is a perfect dish for those homecanned tomatoes. Don't forget the "butter" - it is the secret ingredient.

2 T. oil to sauté
1 clove garlic, minced
½ small onion, chopped (optional)
1 stalk celery, chopped
2 quart jars canned tomatoes
salt and pepper
1 T. nutritional yeast
1 T. Tamari sauce
1 t. oregano
1 t. basil (fresh if possible)
2 cups milk or light cream
1 T. butter
pesto and 1 cup cooked brown rice (optional)

"It was unanimous that our favorite part of our vacation was our stay at Snug Hollow – the experience was so much more than we ever expected. It was also a nice bonus that we met such nice people while we were here."

Aaron & Mary

Heat oil in saucepan and sauté garlic, onion and celery. Add nutritional yeast and Tamari, stirring to blend. Add tomatoes, pepper, oregano, salt and basil. Cook over low heat to boiling. Remove from heat and puree well in blender. Return to heat and add milk or cream and butter. Stir to blend well and serve. Serves 4-5.

You may add a dollop of pesto to each bowl of this creamy soup or stir in a little rice for a more substantial soup. Of course a sprinkling of your favorite cheese is always delicious in hot tomato soup.

Warm Memories...

"Barbara,

What a blessing it has been to stay at your beautiful Snug Hollow. We have been fed with a lot more than just wonderful food (which it is for sure) but also in the soul. Our children are crazy about you and Hillary, and they have learned so much from you and your land. Thank you for sharing your family, friends, your knowledge, love and time with all of us so generously."

With love, your new friends from Miami,

Nick, Melissa, Michael,
Nicole & Naurin

"Peace being a subjective term, I believe I've found as close to an international definition as it gets: Snug Hollow!

I would guess that November, with its barren trees, browned and dying wild grasses and crisp air, is probably one of the least attractive times to be snuggled in here. But that being said, I find it enchanting…. So quiet. A quiet interrupted only by a variety of Kentucky birds, birds that chose Snug Hollow over the tempting migration to the warmer South.

Snug Hollow manages to wrap you up and hold you in a place thought lost to the modern world. The healthful cuisine that Barbara creates nourishes your physical being and the delicious homemade biscuits and gravy –yum– nourish your soul.

Thanks to my dear friend for treating me to this one-of-a-kind retreat in a Kentucky that I love and a hollow that is newly discovered. We'll be back for a breath of fresh wood smoked air, for the quiet that this modern world so desperately needs, a clarity of mind and if November, the dull, desolate barrenly beautiful month can bring these feelings of peace, can you imagine what Spring, Summer, colorful Autumn or a white Winter day would offer? Let us imagine."

Wendy Burke
Farmington, CT

Entrées and Extras

Eggplant Parmesan

I can't remember anyone leaving a bite on the plate.
This is a tasty way to introduce eggplant
and an elegant dinner for any gathering.

Eggplant
2 medium eggplants
bread crumbs to coat
2 beaten eggs
1 cup milk

Slice eggplant into ¾ inch slices. We serve 2 slices per guest. Beat eggs and milk together. Dip eggplant slices into egg mixture and coat with breadcrumbs. Fry in small amount of hot oil until browned and crisp. Place eggplant slices side by side in large baking dish.

Sauce
mix together in a food processor:
2 large cans organic whole tomatoes
2 T. pesto
3 fresh garlic cloves
hot pepper flakes

Mix thoroughly and pour over eggplant. Sprinkle with grated mozzarella and parmesan. Cover and bake in 375° oven for 30 minutes or until eggplant is bubbly and cheese is browned.

Snug Hollow
Rosemary Braided Bread

Serve with a fresh rosemary, sage and olive oil mixture drizzled over the hot loaf. This bread is our signature dish.

---

1 cup whole wheat flour
3½ cups or more all purpose flour
1½ cups warm water
3 T. active dry yeast
1 t. honey
½ t. lemon juice
⅓ cup olive oil
1 T. salt

Rosemary Mixture
½ cup olive oil
2 T. chopped fresh rosemary
1 T. chopped or rubbed sage

Mix together olive oil and herbs. Pour mixture over hot bread and serve warm.

Preheat oven to 400°. This will make 1 large loaf or 2 small loaves.

In large bowl, combine warm water, yeast, honey, lemon juice, olive oil, salt and whole wheat flour. Stir well and let rest for about 5 minutes.

Add remaining flour a little at a time, stirring to mix well until you have a soft dough. Turn out on a floured board to knead.

Add small amounts of flour and knead for approximately 6 minutes or until you have a soft, pliable dough. Pour a little olive oil in your hands and continue kneading until dough "pops up" when punched. Let rest for about 5 minutes.

Divide dough into three balls. With your hands, roll each section into a long rope (about 12 inches) for 1 large loaf. Braid strands loosely into a loaf. Pinch and tuck ends. Transfer to baking sheet and brush with beaten egg. Let rise for 5 minutes in a warm place. Bake approximately 15 minutes or until lightly golden.

Skillet Cornbread

The secret to delicious cornbread is a black iron skillet. By heating the oil in the skillet and pouring in the batter, you get a scrumptiously crunchy crust.

---

2 eggs, beaten	*2 cups cornmeal (white or yellow)*
1¼ cups buttermilk	*½ t. baking soda*
1 t. salt	*1½ t. baking powder*
⅓ cup oil	

Mix dry ingredients in mixing bowl. Add eggs, milk and 2 T. oil to mix and stir well. Heat remaining oil in a 9 inch black cast iron skillet until smoking (careful). Pour cornbread mix into hot skillet and place in preheated 425° oven.

Now the fun begins. After the cornbread has baked for about 10 minutes, shake to see if the middle is set. If so, remove from oven, working very fast, run a spatula around the sides of the cornbread, lift and flip the pone in the skillet. Return to the oven for another 5 minutes or until baked. When you turn it out it will be golden brown on all sides. DO NOT OVERBAKE!

"A seat at Barbara Napier's table is always a treat. Her food is fresh, full of flavor, and, above all, very satisfying."

— *Betty Terry, food editor,*
Taste of the South magazine

Pesto

This may be the greatest gift from our summer garden. We serve it mixed with pasta and chopped tomatoes with feta cheese, or use it to flavor soups and sauces.

6-7 handsful of basil leaves
4 garlic cloves
¼ cup grated Parmesan cheese

½ cup walnuts
½ cup olive oil
sprinkle of salt

Place basil in food processor along with garlic, Parmesan, walnuts, salt and olive oil. You may add some fresh parsley. Pulse in processor until well blended. Add more oil or a little water to make a nice oily paste.

At this point you may eat it all or put it into freezer bags for winter meals. It will keep well in the refrigerator for up to one week.

Beans and Rice

This was my first attempt to eat vegetarian and it is still my favorite meal.
Served with a crispy cornbread and fresh salad, this is something most everyone
will love. Pass the hot sauce or your homemade salsa. This dish makes a beautiful
presentation, with a variety of colors, textures and tastes.

1 bag pinto or cranberry beans   cumin seed
water   brown rice, cooked
1 can whole tomatoes, crushed   cheese, sharp cheddar or your favorite
salt   broccoli, steamed
nutritional yeast   sour cream
Tamari sauce   chopped green onion and bell pepper

Cook beans according to package directions adding Tamari, nutritional yeast, salt and cumin seed to taste. You may add 1 T olive oil. Cook until tender. Add tomatoes and continue to cook for 20 minutes.

On the plate, layer brown rice, beans, broccoli, cheese, tomatoes, peppers, sour cream and onions.

Pizza

Pizza is a satisfying meal when served with a large fresh salad. The choices of toppings are endless: fresh garlic, caramelized onions, pesto, chopped arugula, fresh or roasted peppers or tomatoes. Go for it!

Snug Hollow bread dough recipe
your choice of pizza sauce
mozzarella cheese
Romano cheese
caramelized onions
your favorite toppings

Preheat oven to 425°. Fry onion slices in small amount of oil until caramelized.

Sprinkle a small amount of corn meal on large pizza pans. Roll out dough on floured board, as thinly as possible. Slide the crust onto the pan, tucking the edges.

Cover pizza with sauce and add your choices of cheeses. For a big bubbly hot pizza we suggest a variety of cheeses.

Add caramelized onions and your favorite toppings such as basil, oregano, mushrooms, peppers, etc. We like red pepper flakes and pesto.

Bake until brown and crispy and serve large slices. Pass some feta cheese mixed with fresh chopped tomatoes and pesto for a real treat.

"Dear Barbara,

Unfortunately my last day but we had a wonderful time. The pizza was heavenly, the tart scrumdiddlyumptious and the pancakes a joy.

Our last three visits were great and we will see you again soon."

Rose

Snug Hollow Salad Dressing

Our salads are straight from the garden most of the year. We add seasonal surprises such as slices of cold watermelon in summer or our canned beets in winter. Our orginal dressing makes our salads a guest favorite. Delicious!!!

⅔ cup olive oil
½ cup Tamari sauce
⅔ cup seasoned rice vinegar
⅔ cup nutritional yeast
1 cup water

Mix all ingredients and shake well. Makes a delicious dressing for vegatable or fruit salads. Stays fresh in a sealed container for several weeks.

Lasagna

Everyone enjoys lasagna. It makes a beautiful dinner.
Fresh basil adds tremendous flavor!

Sauce
2 T. pesto
oregano
2 large cans – whole tomatoes
3 fresh garlic cloves

Lasagna Noodles
I use oven ready lasagna,
it is quick and easy to use.

To make sauce, pour canned tomatoes, pesto, oregano, and fresh garlic into food processor. Mix well.

Cheese Filling
3½–4 cups ricotta cheese
2 eggs beaten

1 cup each mozzarella, parmesan and
extra for layering

Mix ricotta with eggs, mozzarella and parmesan cheeses and put aside. *Optional: fresh or frozen thawed spinach.*

To make lasagna, begin by ladling a thin layer of sauce into an oiled lasagna pan and top with a layer of lasagna noodles. Spread ricotta mixture evenly over noodles and top with sauce. You may add a thin layer of spinach steamed and drained or a layer of fresh pesto.

Cover with layer of cheeses and another noodle layer. Spread on last layer of ricotta and top with sauce, mozzarella and parmesan. I like to add a light sprinkling of nutmeg over the top.

Cover loosely with foil and bake in a hot oven of 400° until bubbly and browned, about 50 minutes. We serve it with a mixture of chopped fresh tomatoes, basil and feta cheese.

"Snug Hollow is a wonderful place to celebrate our 57th wedding anniversary. We sat on the porch and rocked and reminisced and thought of all the places we've been in remote corners of the world– and this ranks among the best. Your gracious hospitality Barbara made us feel so welcomed. Your stories of hanging on to this beautiful mountain valley are an inspiration. Loved the whippoorwills at dusk, the birds at dawn and the peace that fills the valley. We really enjoyed the meals, beautifully served and the beauty and coziness of our bedroom and the whole house. The singing was extra! Thanks, Barbara, for a very special time with you. We'll treasure the memory. We hope to return with family."

Ginny & Wendell Kingsolver

Stuffed Bell Peppers

*This is a great way to use your canned tomatoes and fresh peppers from the garden.
This is a summer favorite and serves 6.*

---

3 bell peppers
1 cup cooked brown rice
1 large sliced onion, sautéed
¾ cup grated cheddar cheese
two 8 oz. cans chopped tomatoes, or your own canned tomatoes
1 T. Liquid Smoke
salt and pepper
basil and oregano
optional: 1 can of black beans, rinsed

Slice peppers in half, remove seeds. Blanch quickly in hot boiling water, remove and drain.

Combine rice, cheese, Liquid Smoke and onions in large bowl and beans if you choose to use them.

In food processor, mix tomatoes, basil and seasonings. Add to rice mixture, reserving ½ sauce for later. Fill each pepper half with rice mixture and put into casserole dish with sides touching. You may fill in around the peppers with extra filling. We prefer to use individual serving dishes.

Pour on remaining tomato sauce, cover loosely and bake until set, about 30 minutes at 375°.

Scalloped Potatoes

We usually dig our potatoes late in the fall. There is always someone to help find these hidden gems.

3 large potatoes, sliced thin
1 small onion, sliced thin
2 T. butter
½ cup milk
salt and pepper
cheddar cheese

Layer sliced potatoes and onions in individual, oiled oven proof dishes. Mix melted butter, a little milk and salt and pepper. Pour over potatoes. Sprinkle on cheddar cheese and bake covered for about 30 minutes at 375°. Bake another 5 minutes uncovered or until browned and bubbly. Serves 4-5.

pea pickin' time

"This has been 'by farm' our favorite Bed and Breakfast experience."

Mike & Carrie Creech
Lexington

Bowtie Pasta with
Lemon Cream Sauce & Snap Peas

12 ounces dry bowtie pasta
2 cups snap peas
7 T. butter
2 T. fresh lemon zest
6 T. fresh lemon juice
2 T. chopped fresh garlic
3 cups heavy whipping cream
½ t. sea salt
½ t. pepper
1½ cups fresh chopped tomatoes
½ cup grated parmesan or Romano cheese
1 T. chopped fresh herbs such as thyme, basil or oregano

Cook pasta according to package directions, drain. Lightly steam snap peas, set aside. In a large skillet over medium/high heat, melt butter. Add lemon zest, juice, garlic and fresh herbs. Stir together and cook for 1 minute. Add cream and bring mixture to a slow boil; turn off heat. Stir in salt and pepper. Add pasta and snap peas, stirring slightly. Transfer to plate and top with chopped tomatoes and a generous sprinkling of cheese.

Canning Day on the Farm

Canning is so much more than just placing fruits or vegetables in jars and following the directions on your canner lid. It's the culmination of winter planning, spring planting and summer harvesting. It's the pride you feel when someone talks about your pretty tomatoes, sitting snug in their

jars, waiting to warm your family with a taste of summer on a cold winter evening. It's a labor of love passed from one generation to another, sparking memories as far back as you can remember.

Canning is a fun family endeavor with my daughter-in-law, Rhonda.

Pasta with Greens & Sundried Tomatoes

*Plant a variety of favorite greens in your fall garden for this tasty dish.
Bright Lights Swiss Chard is the star of the show.*

cooked pasta of your choice
3 cloves of chopped fresh garlic
2 T. olive oil
2 cups water
1 ½ cups chopped sundried tomatoes
3 T. Tamari sauce
2 T. nutritional yeast
½ t. red pepper flakes
feta and parmesan cheese
fresh greens: kale, mustard,
    collards, chard, etc.
salt and pepper

In a saucepan sauté garlic in olive oil. Add water, tomatoes, yeast, pepper flakes and Tamari. Bring to a boil and lower heat. Simmer slowly until tomatoes are soft. This should make a delicious brothy sauce.

Wash and chop mixture of greens. Bring small amount of water in hot skillet to boiling, add greens, cover and steam briefly. Drain. Stir tomato mixture into pasta (reserving a small amount.) Dish onto serving plate and top with greens and extra sauce if needed. Sprinkle with parmesan and feta for an added treat. This makes 4-6 servings.

Macaroni and Cheese

Use any combination of cheeses that suits you. We like to top off the dish with chopped red pimientos. Lovely and tasty.

---

3 T. butter
2 T. flour
1 T. nutritional yeast
1 lb. macaroni - cooked al denté
1 cup of sharp cheddar
   or any mixture of cheeses (grated)
1 cup of parmesan (grated)
1 sliced onion, caramelized
1½ cups milk or light cream
coarse sea salt and pepper
1 cup sour cream

Make a roux of butter and flour by stirring together in a skillet over medium heat. When roux is golden, whisk in 1 cup milk or cream and stir constantly until boiling. Add salt and lots of pepper.

"My husband picked the spot and told me it didn't have central heat. I told him to keep looking and like any good husband he forgot. Boy am I glad he didn't listen to me! We have so enjoyed our stay here. It's been like having our very own mountain retreat. So relaxing, so beautiful, so peaceful and so what we wanted. Thanks for everything."

Gina & Eric
Texas

Add macaroni and mix all ingredients together with ½ cup milk or enough to make mixture wet. Stir to blend. Pour into casserole dish or individual serving dishes. Sprinkle generously with buttered bread crumbs, (we use our rosemary breadcrumbs). Bake at 450° until crumbs are toasty and cheese is bubbly, about 15 minutes.

Quick Cheese Soufflés

We serve these tasty individual soufflés with our homemade vegetable soup.

2-3 T. butter

3 T. flour

3 eggs, separated

1½ cups mixture of crumbled
    cheeses (we use feta and parmesan)

pinch of salt and pepper

pinch of fresh rosemary
    or herb of your choice

1¼ cups milk

Position rack to middle of oven and preheat to 425°. Beat egg yolks and whites separately. Melt butter in a saucepan and add flour. Make roux by stirring until browned and add milk and herbs. Stirring constantly, add yolks and cook until thick, about 3 minutes. Remove from heat, add cheese mixture and stir well. Fold in egg whites. Pour into buttered ramekins or you may use one large dish. Place ramekins in a large baking pan and pour in boiling water that comes half-way up the side of the ramekins. Bake for 20-25 minutes, or until puffed and brown. Should make 4-6 individual servings.

Quiche

Perfect for dinner and summer lunches. An heirloom tomato's best friend.
You can use any combination of cheeses.

Quiche Crust
1¼ cups flour
6 T. butter
¼ t. salt
2 T. water
a squirt of lemon juice

Crust: Mix dry ingredients and butter in food processor. Add lemon juice and water. If needed, add a little more water and continue mixing until crumbly. Press crust into pie pan or tart pan with removable bottom. Bake in a preheated oven at 400° until set, about 5-8 minutes.

Quiche Filling

3 eggs	*herbs and nutmeg*
1 cup heavy cream	*1 T. minced celery and onion*
¼ cup milk	*salt and pepper to taste*
¼ cup sour cream	*1½ cups diced cheese*
	(cheddar, Swiss, Monterey Jack, Asiago)

Quiche: Sauté onion and celery in small amount of butter and spread on crust. Sprinkle on herbs such as oregano and basil and cover with cheese. Beat eggs slightly. Mix with cream, milk, salt and pepper. Pour over cheese. Bake in a 350° oven about 10 minutes or until set and lightly browned.

In summer, we add thinly sliced tomatoes after pouring in the egg mixture. This makes a beautiful cold entrée. Add a dollop of fresh pesto and serve with a big summer salad.

Barbecued Tofu

Tofu that has been frozen has a nice chewy texture. You may use bottled barbecue sauce if you don't want to make your own.

Freeze and thaw 1 block firm tofu. Gently squeeze water from tofu block and let rest on paper towel for a few minutes to drain. Cut into 1" slices. Preheat oven to 350°.

Mix together:

¼ cup oil	*2 T. Tamari sauce*
2 T. chunky peanut butter	*2 T. nutritional yeast*
¼ t. black pepper	

Pour mixture over tofu, covering each slice. Let marinate for 30 minutes, turning to coat well. Arrange tofu slices in large, flat, greased casserole dish. Bake for about 20 minutes or until lightly browned. Turn pieces over and continue to bake until crispy.

Barbeque Sauce:

In oil, sauté onion, Tamari and garlic until translucent. Add remaining ingredients and simmer about 20 minutes.

⅓ cup oil	*salt and pepper*
1 large onion, sliced	*2 T. Liquid Smoke*
1 T. Tamari	*1 t. allspice*
1 T. nutritional yeast	*2 T. yellow mustard*
2 cups thick tomato sauce	*1 T. molasses*
⅓ cup water	*¾ cup brown sugar*
1 T. finely chopped garlic	

Pour sauce over baked tofu slices and continue to bake for 15 minutes or more to get sauce simmering.

Corn Fritters

A favorite childhood memory was a visit to my Aunt Emily's farm in the middle of summer. She cooked a big dinner (lunch, really, but in the mountains we call it dinner). After a hot trip to her overgrown garden, she made these and called them gritted bread.

---

corn on the cob (a little too ripe)
butter
flour
salt
oil for frying

Remove husks and wash corn. Grate the corn kernel from the cob with a food grater. Milk the cobs by running a knife over them to let the juice run into the bowl. Mix in a little flour and salt to make a soft mixture. Fry in hot oil until crispy. The centers will be soft and have a burst of corn flavor you won't believe!

"The singing stream, talking birds and calming breeze.
The curios, the books, the nooks and crannies, every space a
*   story to be told.*
Candlelight and setting sun to light up the most nourishing
*   and delicious meals.*
Above all...the peace – healing, healing, whole!
And dogs too!!!

Many thanks and looking forward to our next visit. "

Michael Connelly
California

Roasted Spring & Summer Vegetables

Roasting vegetables requires a hot oven. High heat brings out the juices and makes the vegetables crisp. Don't be tempted to over-stir the vegetables. Use a spatula to quickly turn once.

2 medium summer squash or zucchini
4 small red or Yukon gold potatoes
1 red bell pepper
1 green bell pepper
2-3 handfuls beans (whole)
2-3 large onions and carrots
5-6 whole garlic cloves
⅓ cups olive oil
3 T. Tamari sauce
nutritional yeast
fresh herbs such as oregano, summer savory
salt and pepper

Slice squash in half, remove seeds and cut into quarters. Thickly slice or chop remaining vegetables, leaving the beans whole. Place vegetables in a large bowl and add olive oil, Tamari sauce and herbs, salt and pepper to taste. Stir until coated well. Spread vegetables on a large baking sheet and roast in a 450° oven until browned, about 25 minutes. Stir to loosen from bottom and to ensure all vegetables brown well.

Vegetable Pot Pies

Served with fried apples, roasted Brussels sprouts and a side of cranberry sauce; this is a perfect winter dinner. The sage and thyme lend themselves to Christmas or Thanksgiving tastes.

¼ cup flour	½ cup cooked lentils
2 T. butter	1 t. dried thyme and sage
1 large chopped onion	2 cups frozen chopped vegetables
1 t. salt	¼ t. nutmeg
freshly ground pepper	1 qt. milk
1 cup cheddar, shredded	2 cups frozen peas

Make biscuits from the Snug Hollow Biscuits recipe to top the pie.

In a skillet, make a roux by whisking flour into butter over medium heat. Cook until lightly browned. Add onion, nutmeg, salt, pepper, thyme and sage; cook onion until it becomes translucent, about 2 minutes. Stir in milk and heat mixture to boiling. Reduce heat and simmer, stirring constantly until thick, about 6 minutes. Remove from heat, add cheese and lentils. Stir until melted. Add frozen peas and mixed vegetables to cheese sauce.

Pour filling into individual serving dishes and top with 1 or 2 small biscuits. Sprinkle with sage. Arrange dishes on large cookie sheet and bake until biscuits are browned and filling is bubbly. About 40 minutes at 400°. Makes 4-6 servings.

Roasted Winter Vegetables

Roasting brings out the natural sweetness of vegetables. The crisp outer layer is juicy and a real taste treat. A fast and easy dish to prepare and you can be so creative using most anything from your garden. At Snug Hollow we serve them alongside our Kentuscan Bean soup and cheese grits or to compliment the fresh spinach lasagna. The vegetables are tasty cold or heated and can be served the next day with a tomato quiche. This is a fast and easy dish.

⅓ cups olive oil

6-7 whole garlic cloves

3 large carrots

2 T. Tamari sauce

3 large onions

2 turnips

1 large sweet potato or butternut squash

fresh herbs such as rosemary,
    sage, thyme, salt and pepper

4 small red or Yukon gold potatoes

2 cups Brussels sprouts or broccoli

2-3 beets

Quarter onions and thickly slice vegetables except Brussels sprouts and broccoli. Mix the vegetables except the green ones in a large bowl. Add olive oil, Tamari sauce, herbs, salt and pepper to taste. Stir until coated well with oil. Spread vegetables on a large baking sheet and roast in a 425° oven until vegetables begin to brown (about 20 minutes). Stir and turn once during roasting to loosen from pan and ensure even browing. Coat Brussels sprouts and broccoli with oil, add to pan and roast about 20 minutes or until done. These vegetables will be quite brown, crisp and delicious!

Snug Hollow's piece of the "Quilt Trail"

Pasta and Stir-Fried Vegetables

One of my favorite dinners, this entree is made of fresh seasonal vegetables, quickly stir fried with garlic and olive oil and served over pasta. Spring/summer may bring us crisp green beans, peas, onions, summer squash, peppers, basil and tomatoes. Fall/winter offers butternut squash, mustard greens, beets, Swiss chard, basil and onions.

Heat a small amount of olive oil in a deep skillet and add the washed, chopped vegetables. Let them cook until tender stirring to keep them from burning (may add small amount of water to steam winter vegetables). In another pan, heat olive oil, chopped garlic, Tamari and simmer. Pour over drained vegetables.

Cook pasta and drain. Toss pasta with brown butter or garlic and olive oil. Serve vegetables over pasta with fresh chopped tomatoes.

snappin' peas on the porch

Spring New Potatoes
with Creamy Cheese Sauce

12 –15 small new potatoes   2 T. flour
1½ cups milk or buttermilk   ½ t. salt or to taste
1t. pepper   2 T. butter

Wash and steam potatoes. Drain.

Cream Sauce:

In a saucepan make a roux by heating butter until sizzling and add flour, salt and pepper, stirring well until browned. Whisk in milk and cheese and stir until well blended and sauce begins to thicken. Pour over potatoes and serve. You may add a sprinkling of chopped herbs and parsley.

Fried Okra

Fried okra is my favorite summer dish and a chance to use our locally ground cornmeal. I remember my first gardening endeavor when my sister and I grew okra. We didn't realize that it kept producing and unfortunately cut it down after our first harvest. I've come a long way in my gardening and now my "okra patch" is a thing of beauty and supplies a bounty of okra for weeks. The delicate yellow flowers are a treat in themselves.

cornmeal to coat okra
3 cups thinly sliced okra
oil for frying

Slice okra into thin pieces. Sprinkle cornmeal, salt and pepper over okra to coat. Pour into hot oil and fry until golden brown. Stir often. Drain and serve. Serves 3-4.

Smashed Potatoes

red or Yukon gold potatoes
evaporated milk
sea salt and pepper
butter

Cut potatoes into large chunks, cover with water and cook over low heat until soft. We don't usually peel our potatoes since they are our own and grown organically. Drain potatoes, add milk, salt, pepper and butter. The evaporated milk is a must! Please, use it lavishly. Using a potato masher, smash potatoes until chunky. Stir and serve.

a guest enjoys an afternoon of cookbook reading at its best

Caramelized Onions

Caramelized onions on pasta with brown butter and Romano cheese is a hit.

Slice onions into thick slices. Place onion slices in a large heavy skillet with a small amount of olive oil. Cook on low heat for an hour or until nicely browned, stirring occasionally. These onions can be used in so many ways. I add them to our homemade pizzas, as a layer in lasagna, mixed in stir fried greens, or Brussels sprouts. You may want to add a few garlic cloves near the end and mix with brown butter.

Green Beans

thin beans
olive oil
chopped garlic
Tamari sauce

Wash beans and remove ends and strings. Steam until al dente and drain.

In a skillet, heat a small amount of olive oil and chopped garlic and simmer for a minute. Add Tamari and beans, stirring until hot and coated. Turn off heat, cover skillet for about 5 minutes and serve.

strangely enough, most times our green beans are yellow

Fried Sweet Potatoes

peanut or canola oil
butter
sugar
thinly sliced sweet potatoes (2 potatoes equal one serving)

Heat small amount of oil and butter in a large flat skillet, add potatoes, sprinkle with sugar and cover. Fry over medium heat until crisp on the bottom, then turn over and cook until crisp. Salt if needed. Serve drizzled with warm molasses.

Stir-Fried Fresh Greens

Fresh greens of any kind melt down to less than half their size when cooked. Remember to have lots on hand if you are preparing several servings. I like to add a few red pepper flakes. Great compliment to macaroni cheese.

---

chopped garlic

green onions

kale, mustard, collards, chard and
  broccoli raab (makes a good mixture)

Tamari sauce

olive oil

Wash well and chop a mixture of greens and green onions. Bring to a boil a small amount of water in skillet and add greens, cover and steam briefly. Drain. In a separate skillet, heat a small amount of olive oil, chopped garlic and Tamari and allow to simmer for a couple of minutes. Add greens to hot mixture and serve.

Baked Hubbard Squash

This dish is a delightful surprise with its smooth and flavorful taste. The golden color is wonderful. We serve this as a side dish to our pasta with brown butter.

1 large hubbard or butternut squash
curry powder
cinnamon
cayenne pepper (a smidgeon)
brown sugar
molasses

Remove seeds and cut squash into serving size chunks. No need to peel, it gets very soft. Arrange in a large oiled baking pan. Sprinkle with spices, sugar and molasses. Add a bit of water to pan. Cover and bake at medium heat until done.

Brown Butter

Brown butter is delicious on pasta, vegetables, or mixed with carmalized onions.

In a heavy skillet, melt 2 sticks of butter over medium heat, stirring occasionally. Let butter melt and begin to cook over very low heat. When the butter separates and turns lightly brown, remove from heat. For a stronger taste you may add a little sage to the butter as it cooks. I prefer to add a little sea salt at this point. This may be kept in the refrigerator for up to a week.

Brussels Sprouts - Brenda's Way

We can never make enough of this! Even our guests who say they don't like Brussels sprouts will end up eating the last one!

---

1 quart Brussels sprouts
1 large chopped onion
2 cloves garlic - finely chopped

1 T. Tamari sauce
2 T. nutritional yeast

Wash and remove outer leaves from Brussels sprouts. Reserve outer leaves.

Heat skillet with small amount of olive oil. When hot, add outer leaves of Brussels sprouts, chopped onion and garlic. Sauté until onions are translucent and Brussels sprouts leaves are beginning to brown.

Add Brussels sprouts and stir-fry briefly until starting to brown. Add Tamari and yeast. Cover and cook until fork tender.

good food and conversation can always be found in the kitchen

Lazy afternoons
on the farm

Desserts

Fresh Strawberry Pie

In late May and early June, we pick strawberries in Kentucky for pies, jams, shortcakes and eating by the handsful. Served with freshly whipped cream, it makes a scrumptious summer dessert. This recipe also makes beautiful individual tarts.

---

2 T. melted butter
1 T. sugar
9" short crust shell, baked
fresh whole strawberries, enough to fill crust

Pat short crust into a 9" tart pan with removable bottom. Bake at 375°, approximately 7-10 minutes until lightly browned. While pie crust is hot from the oven, sprinkle it with melted butter and sugar. Set aside to cool.

Strawberry Glaze
1 cup sugar or honey	*2½ T. cornstarch*
1 T. red wine vinegar	*1 T. butter*
½ cup water	*2 cups strawberries (measured before crushing)*

Crush berries in food processor. Mix with remaining ingredients. Cook and stir over medium heat until clear, about 5 minutes. Let cool. Fill crust with whole berries and pour glaze over fruit. Chill and serve.

"What a lovely weekend. The storm last night was amazing and watching/experiencing the dawn and clearing sky was like witnessing the creation. Thanks for sharing."

Jim B.
Louisville

Short Crust

We use our short crust recipe for fruit pies and tarts. This also makes buttery cookies to serve with ice cream and gingered peaches.

1¼ cups all purpose flour
¼ t. salt
¼ cup powdered sugar
7 T. butter
water

Combine all ingredients in a food processor. Pulse and add enough water (about 3 T.) until it begins to stick together. Pour into pie pan, tart pan or cake pan, depending on what you are making. Using floured fingers, lightly press onto bottom and sides of pan. I usually bake this crust first for fruit desserts. For an old fashioned fruit pie, roll out the shortcrust on a floured surface, a little larger than the pie pan. Fit the crust into the pan with the edges hanging over. Pour in your filling and fold the edges toward the middle to cover the filling. Sprinkle with sugar and cinnamon or cloves and bake at 350° until nicely browned and bubbly.

We serve our pies in many different sizes and shapes. My Tater Knob Pottery pie bakers are a favorite for fruit pies. They are beautiful and come in a variety of sizes and colors.

Sara's Tater Knob Pottery and Studio is right up the road. It is a fun place to spend the afternoon.

For a tangy combination of summer fruits, combine blackberries, blueberries, rhubarb, peaches and strawberries. Substitute equal amounts of each fruit to make up the called for amount and bake as any fruit pie. Crème fraîche and ice cream are perfect toppings.

A fruit pie usually requires a top crust. When you add a top crust, leave an opening for steam to escape. For a detailed pie "how to", refer to an old standby, such as the *Joy of Cooking*.

Individual tart pans with removable bottoms come in all shapes and sizes. These heart shaped strawberry tarts are our favorite.

My Mom's Pecan Pie

Thanksgiving and Christmas dinners always include Mom's pecan pie. You could add a few fresh cranberries before baking.

1 cup sugar
½ cup dark corn syrup
¼ cup butter
3 whole eggs
¼ t. salt
1 T. vinegar
1 cup pecans
1 t. vanilla
1 T. flour
short crust recipe

this pie is a hit at special dinners ...

Combine all ingredients in a saucepan and heat until boiling, stirring well. Bake pie crust for 10 minutes at 350°. Pour in filling and continue to bake in moderate oven at 350° for about 30 minutes or until set.

....and a Red Hat favorite.

Brenda's Butterscotch Pie

My sister Brenda shared this recipe with me. Snug Hollow parties often include this pie and guests leave with the recipe. There's always a rush for the last piece.

---

2 cups brown sugar, lightly packed
8 T. cornstarch
2 pinches salt
6 egg yolks
4 cups evaporated milk
1 stick butter
1 T. vanilla
1 T. maple flavoring

In a heavy saucepan mix sugar, salt and cornstarch. Beat egg yolks into ½ of the milk and add to sugar mixture. Cook over medium heat, adding remaining milk. Cook, stirring constantly, until thickened (will get lumpy at first, but then smooth out). Do not overcook.

Remove from heat and add butter and flavorings. Mix well to melt butter and smooth mixture. Pour into 8" or 9" baked pie shell. (Makes 2 - 8" pies)

Meringue

Beat 6 egg whites with electric mixer, until meringue holds soft peaks. Add 12 T. sugar (2 per egg) by two tablespoonfuls at a time and continue to beat until meringue holds stiff peaks. Fold in 1 t. vanilla. Spread liberally on hot pie filling, sealing well around edges of crust. Bake at 450° for 10-15 minutes until browned.

Chocolate Tart

I found this recipe at the Arbor House Inn in Madison, Wisconsin while visiting friends. On our side of the mountain at Snug Hollow, it has become a guest favorite.

Short Crust

1¼ cups all purpose flour	3 T. cold water
¼ cup powdered sugar	7 T. chilled butter
¼ t. salt	

To prepare the crust combine flour, sugar and salt in bowl of a food processor. Cut in chilled butter using pulse button. Add cold water and blend to make dry dough. May need to add a little more water one teaspoon at a time.

Using floured hands, lightly press into bottom and sides of 9" tart pan with removable bottom. Bake about 15 minutes in preheated 375° oven until it begins to brown.

Filling
1 cup plus 2 T. bittersweet or semisweet chocolate morsels
6 T. butter
2 large eggs
¼ cup sugar
2 T. light corn syrup
1 T. espresso powder, (finely ground coffee beans)
½ cup chopped walnuts or pecans

In a small saucepan over low heat, melt chocolate and butter. Set aside. In a medium bowl, beat eggs well. Add sugar, corn syrup, espresso powder and salt to eggs and whisk together. Stir in butter and chocolate mixture and chopped nuts. Stir one final time and pour into partially baked pie crust. Bake for 15 minutes at 375°, or until center is set. Let tart cool and remove from tart pan. Serve warm with ice cream or a dollop of freshly whipped cream.

Mom's Chocolate Cake

Unbelievably delicious! Mom made 7 minute frosting, but we are not that ambitious.
Kim makes this cake without chocolate for a most interesting spice cake.

4 squares unsweetened chocolate, melted
1 cup butter
2 cups sugar
2 cups all purpose flour
1 t. soda
½ t. cinnamon
½ t. allspice
1 t. nutmeg
pinch salt
5 whole eggs
1 cup buttermilk
2 t. vanilla

my mom, aka Granny, our free
cooking consultant in the holler.

Cream together butter and sugar using an electric mixer. Add eggs, one at a time, to butter sugar mixture, beating until mixed well.

Combine dry ingredients in a bowl. In a separate bowl combine buttermilk and vanilla. Alternately add dry ingredients and buttermilk mixture to egg mixture, blending well. Add chocolate and mix well.

Pour into greased and floured pans and bake at 325° for 35-40 minutes. Makes three 8 inch layers.

Rhondell's Jalapeno Pepper Jelly

Rhondell has become a good friend over her years as a guest at the farm. After trying her hand at gardening, she shares her garden goodies with me. This pepper jelly is the best ever.

¾ pound jalapeno peppers.
(a large mess will do)
2 cups cider vinegar, divided
2 pouches liquid pectin
6 cups sugar

Wash peppers and drain.* Remove stems and seeds. (If you want it a little hot, leave a few seeds and also add a few cayenne peppers). Puree peppers and 1 cup vinegar in a food processor or blender. Combine puree, 2nd cup vinegar and sugar in a large saucepot. Bring to a boil; boil 10 minutes, stirring constantly. Stir in liquid pectin. Return to a rolling boil. Boil hard 1 minute, stirring onstantly. Remove from heat. Skim foam if necessary. Ladle hot jelly into hot jars, leaving ¼-inch headspace. Adjust two-piece lids. Process 10 minutes in a boiling water canner.

Be sure to wear rubber gloves when you are cutting and seeding the hot peppers.

"I am a new organic gardener thanks to Barbara. After my first visit to Snug Hollow in November 2007, she began to give me great and practical tips on the simplicity of organic gardening.

Last season I was able to put up enough food by canning/freezing for my family of 3 for the year even though my garden is small and compact.

One of the best things I learned was how to group together my plantings and not think about rows but small plots. To cut down on weeds, my garden was grown in hills and mulched with straw. To fertilize, Barbara recommended fish fertilizer. The smell is awful but the results are wonderful.

I would check the garden daily for any "bad" insects and I used an organic wash when I needed to "debug" the garden. Barbara also recommended using a hot pepper spray to deter the bugs.

My family now buys all of our meat and dairy from local farmers. What we do not grow we get at the local farmer's market in Charleston. Food for thought; Grow a row to take to your local food pantry or soup kitchen!"

Rhondell Miller
Sissonville, WV

Artists at work...

...on the farm

Aunt Nora's Cheese Straws

Rhonda's Aunt Nora would be proud of her Cheese Straws' popularity.
These are a family favorite. A sort of recipe-in-law!

¾ lb. shredded sharp cheddar cheese
1 stick butter at room temperature
1 t. baking powder
¾ t. salt
1⅔ cups all purpose flour, more if needed
cayenne pepper

Sift and measure 1 cup flour with baking powder and salt. Mix cheese and butter, then add as much flour mixture as needed to make stiff dough.

Using thinnest ribbon attachment, use a cookie press to process dough into 2-3 inch strips onto an oiled baking sheet. Sprinkle with cayenne pepper to taste. Bake in 400° oven for 10 minutes, or until light golden brown. Watch closely! Makes about 3 dozen.

Rhonda Welch's Jam Cake

I prefer the cake without raisins and nuts, although we serve it both ways.
Sometimes we bake small loaves and use a caramel icing when we bake a large cake.

1¾ cups all purpose flour

1½ cups sugar

1 cup oil

1 cup buttermilk

3 eggs

1 cup raisins

1 cup walnuts

½ t. salt

1 t. ground cloves

1 t. nutmeg

1 t. allspice

1 t. vanilla

1 t. baking soda

1½ cups blackberry jam
   (we prefer jam with seeds)

Mix all ingredients except nuts and raisins. Beat at high speed for 8 minutes. Fold nuts and raisins into mixture. Bake at 350° for 40 minutes in two 9 inch greased and flour dusted cake pans.

"This was a great, unique weekend get-away for our wedding anniversary. Barbara gave us the perfect mix of solitude and comfortable chat. We enjoyed the friendly conversation with other guests the night we had dinner (served on the porch with an accompanying cool breeze) and the delicious breakfasts. All the food was lovingly prepared using fresh ingredients. The setting is like no other B&B we have stayed in and getting here is half the adventure! We look forward to the opportunity for a return visit."

Ursula and Bob
Washington, D.C.

Vicki's Coconut Cake

This southern favorite is the supreme birthday or anniversary cake.
My friend, Vicki Spurlock, baked this as a wedding cake adorned with fresh flowers.
I always serve it to the travel writers when they visit the farm. It sure gets their interest.

Coconut Cake

1⅓ cups sugar	2 eggs	4 t. baking powder
½ cup butter	3 cups flour	2 t. vanilla
1 cup milk	½ t. salt	

In a small mixing bowl, cream together sugar and eggs until fluffy. Sift together flour, salt and baking powder into a separate bowl. Add flour mixture to the egg mixture alternately with the milk. Beat with mixer at medium speed for 2 minutes. Pour into 2 greased and floured 9 inch round cake pans. Bake for 350 degrees for 30-40 minutes, or until it test done. When cool, split layers.

Coconut Filling

2 cups sugar	2 cups milk	12 ounces flake coconut
¼ cup flour	4 eggs, beaten	1 t. coconut extract
	1 t. vanilla extract	

In a heavy bottom saucepan, mix together milk and sugar. Whisk in flour and cook over low heat, stirring constantly until boiling. Add eggs and continue stirring and cooking. Let boil for 1 minute. Remove from heat and stir in coconut and flavorings. Let cool. Place first cake layer on serving plate and begin filling the four layers as you stack the cake. Remove all crumbs before icing.

Icing: Whip 2 cups heavy whipping cream with ¼ cup powdered sugar until soft peaks forms. The icing should be whipped enough for spreading. Refrigerate for at least 20 minutes to chill. Ice the cake just before serving. Enjoy!

Sweet Cream Pound Cake

Laura Dennis has been a helpful friend of Snug Hollow since her high school days. She is now a registered dietician and a wonderful cook. She introduced her cake for a summer birthday celebration on the farm.

½ lb. butter, softened

3 cups sugar

6 eggs

3 ¼ cups all-purpose flour

½ pt. whipping cream

1 t. vanilla (or pure maple flavoring)

1 t. lemon juice

In a medium mixing bowl, cream butter and sugar until smooth. To this mixture, add one egg at a time and beat two minutes after each egg. With mixer on low, add ½ of the flour. Slowly add whipping cream, lemon juice and vanilla. Add remainder of the flour and mix well. Pour into a buttered tube pan and bake 1 hour and 20 minutes at 325°.

coconut cake

Meg's Hot Chocolate Truffles

You will need a pair of disposable gloves for this. The chilies can be hot!

Filling

1 lb. dark chocolate (5 bars/5 cups chips)
  the higher % the cocoa, the better

3 T. unsalted butter

½ cup heavy whipping cream

2-3 oz. liqueur (Kahlua, Grand Marnier,
mint, bourbon, etc.) optional

1 T. ground ancho chilies powder

½ t. cayenne powder

Coating

½ lb. milk chocolate (3 bars or
  3 cups chips)

chopped nuts, cocoa powder,
  coconut, etc.

Wearing gloves, prepare the ancho chilies by cutting off stems with scissors. Cut lengthwise. Empty out seeds and cut into inch sized pieces. Put into a coffee grinder and grind until powdery. You may add a little espresso powder. Melt 1 lb. dark chocolate at a very low setting in a double boiler. It is best if the temperature stays just below 130°. Stir in separately: butter, whipping cream, liqueur, ancho chilies and cayenne pepper.

After all ingredients are thoroughly mixed, transfer to a freezer container. Let cool on the counter, then cover and put in freezer to harden.

When filling is hard, use a tough spoon to scoop into spoonfuls. Your scoops will not be perfect, but you may roll into small balls with your palms. Place balls on a parchment covered baking sheet.

After chocolate balls are formed, begin melting your milk chocolate slowly and keep it just under 130°. When melted, dip and swirl your chocolate balls quickly, until fully covered. Do this with a large metal spoon. Once covered, lift out and place on baking sheet. Sprinkle with your choice of nuts, cocoa, coconut, etc. The truffles will harden immediately. You may serve these or freeze them. Yields 16 truffles.

Brenda's Egg Custard

To serve this custard, use that beautiful glass pitcher your grandma gave you. This recipe requires lots of stirring while cooking.

---

1 quart milk
4 – 6 eggs
¾ – 1 cup sugar
pinch of salt
2 t. vanilla (or more to taste)

Pour milk into a large heavy-bottomed saucepan. Cook over medium heat to scald. While milk heats, beat sugar and salt into eggs until well mixed. Temper egg mixture by stirring in a cup of warm milk. Pour into the saucepan with remaining milk. Cook and stir constantly over low heat until mixture coats the back of a spoon.

DO NOT OVERCOOK - DO NOT BOIL!!!

Remove from heat and plunge into icy water bath until cool or at least room temp. Add vanilla and strain into container. Refrigerate. (if mixture has curdled, use electric hand mixer or blender to smooth)

Using 4 eggs makes a thin, drinkable custard. Custard thickens as it cools.

Dad's Old Fashioned Apple Stack Cake

Apple Stack Cake is an old Kentucky favorite. Dried apples used in this dessert are usually found in rural Kentucky and are treasures that are hard to come by. I remember as a child, kitchens decorated with strings of sliced apples drying in sunny windows.

Cooked Dried Apples:

In a heavy saucepan, add 5 cups of dried apples, 1 cup white sugar, 1 cup brown sugar and 5 cups water. Add spices such as ground nutmeg, cinnamon and cloves to taste. Cover and cook over low heat, adding more water as needed. Apples should cook down to a very thick sauce. Stir often to prevent scorching. Let cool.

Stack Cakes

½ cup butter	3½ cups all purpose flour
½ cup sugar	2 t. baking powder
⅓ cup molasses	½ t. salt
1 egg, beaten	1 t. ground ginger
½ cup buttermilk	1 t. vanilla

Cream together sugar and butter; add egg, molasses and buttermilk. Mix well. Sift flour, salt, soda and ginger and add to egg mixture. Mix well and add vanilla. This makes a firm dough. With floured hands, pat dough into a 9 inch round cake pan. This recipe should make 6 rounds. Bake at 350° for 10 minutes. When the cake is cool, stack the layers with cooled dried apples. This cake needs to rest for a few hours before serving.

Snug Hollow Apple Dumplings

Dumplings
use Snug Hollow Biscuit Recipe
3-4 medium apples
brown sugar, cinnamon, nutmeg,
sugar and water

Make biscuit recipe and roll dough into balls (the size of a plum). Roll out each ball on floured board making a thin circle of pastry. Add to the center ¼ cup of diced apples per dumpling. (No need to peel if they are organic.) Add generous sprinkling of brown sugar/cinnamon/nutmeg mixture, about 2 T. per dumpling. Fold dough over apples to make envelope style dumplings, sealing edges well and transfer to greased baking dish. I use a floured spatula to transfer delicate pastries.

My mother made apple dumplings on wash day, or at least that is my memory. The heavenly scent of baking apples and nutmeg calls our guests to the table real fast. We serve them with a little fresh cream for dinner desserts and breakfast treats. Our apple trees were planted 30 years ago, seedlings from my Aunt Gladys' farm. In the fall we gather bushels of apples. leaving some to share with the deer and crows.

Sauce
bring to a boil
3 cups water	*2 cups sugar*
2 T. butter	*1 T. ground nutmeg*

Pour sugar and water mixture over and around dumplings. Bake at 400° for about 15 minutes or until dumplings are browned. Serve with a splash of lightly whipped cream and extra sauce. Makes 4 servings.

REAL Chocolate Pie

This is a real homemade chocolate pie. The honey makes it "really" delicious!

2⅓ cups evaporated milk

3 egg yolks slightly beaten

2 T. butter

1 scant cup honey

3 squares unsweetened chocolate, cut into pieces

5 level T. flour

1 t. vanilla extract

¼ t. salt

½ t. maple flavoring

Preheat oven to 400°. Prepare and bake 8 inch pie shell, cool.

Filling: in medium saucepan combine honey, flour, chocolate and salt. Mix well with whisk. Stir in cream, mixing until smooth. Bring to boiling over medium heat, stirring; boil 1 minute stirring constantly. Remove from heat.

Stir half of hot mixture into yolks and mix well. Pour back into saucepan. Return to a boil, stirring constantly. Boil 1 minute. Remove from heat and add butter. Stir in extracts and pour into baked crust.

Meringue

3 egg whites at room temperature

¼ t. cream of tarter

6 T. sugar

drop of vanilla flavoring

drop of maple flavoring

In medium bowl, with electric mixer beat egg whites and cream of tartar until soft peaks form. Gradually beat in sugar 2 T. at a time, beating after each addition. Add vanilla and maple flavoring and continue beating until stiff peaks form. Spread meringue over warm filling, sealing meringue to edges of crust and swirling.

Bake at 400° for 7 to 10 minutes or until meringue is golden. Cool on wire rack.

Rhubarb / Cherry Pie

Rhubarb, sometimes called pie plant, is a new taste to many of our guests. It has been around for a long time, showing up in many farm gardens or by the kitchen door. Rhubarb / Cherry pie is a local favorite. Strawberries can be used instead of cherries.

¾ cup sugar

pinch of ground cloves and cinnamon

½ cup brown sugar

3 T. minute tapioca

⅛ t. salt

4½ cups tart pitted cherries or 2 cans

1 cup sliced fresh rhubarb (¾ inch pieces)

2 T. butter

cedar waxwing in our cherry tree

Drain cherries, reserving 1 cup juice.

Mix together sugars, cloves, tapioca, butter and salt in saucepan; mix in cherry juice. Bring to a boil, stirring and reduce heat. Simmer about 4 minutes until slightly thickened.

Stir in rhubarb/fruit and pour into pie shell.

You may use a conventional pie crust, but I prefer our crispy, buttery short crust. For this pie you may roll out the short crust on a floured board to fit any 8 inch pan you like. I prefer to roll the dough larger than the pie pan. I place it in the pie pan, pour in the filling, dot with butter and lightly fold the crust over to cover. Sprinkle the crust with sugar and cinnamon. Bake at 425° for 30 to 35 minutes until golden brown.

Blackberry Pie

In summer, the farm fields are full of juicy, sweet blackberries ready for the adventurous picker. The effort is well worth the time, despite the chiggers and poison ivy.

"Dear Barbara,

When I got here I had been on the road for six days and was mighty weary. This morning after sleeping in this Kentucky dream of a home, I'm rejuvenated body and soul.

The food, excellent. The company, perfectly marvelous and the surroundings - priceless. You have found an Eden here. Thank you for sharing it with others - especially with me."

Wanda McKinny,
Southern Living Magazine

For one 8" pie
5 cups blackberries, fresh or frozen (thawed)
1 cup sugar
¼ cup flour
2 T. butter
1 t. lemon juice

Carefully stir together all ingredients except butter and pour into unbaked pie shell. Top with small pieces of the butter. This pie needs a top crust so you may roll it out or fold over (see page 36). Sprinkle top crust with sugar /cinnamon mixture and bake 40-45 minutes at 425° until brown and juice is bubbly. Serves 6 to 8.

Holiday Eggnog

Snug Hollow wedding party

Our eggnog goes well with Kentucky Bourbon and we serve extra nutmeg on the side.
This is a special holiday treat for our guests as they warm by the fire and watch it snow.
This recipe was given to me by my son's elementary school principal.
The eggs are uncooked, so use your own discretion.

The day before serving, separate 2 dozen eggs. Mix yolks with 2 cups sugar, 1 t. nutmeg and 2 t. vanilla. Stir well or shake thoroughly. Cover and refrigerate overnight.

Before serving, beat egg whites until stiff and whip 1 quart whipping cream. Mix yolks with 2 cups milk, fold in beaten whites and whipped cream. Avoid too much stirring. Ladle carefully into your favorite pitcher.

Your Notes and Recipes

Index

Breakfast

Soups

Entrées and Extras

Desserts

Cozy Cabin

Planning Your Visit

Snuggled in the mountains of Kentucky, Snug Hollow Farm Bed & Breakfast invites guests to enjoy their Kentucky experience from the heart of the state. This 300 acre secluded retreat is an original **Kentucky Farm Stay** and member of **Eco-friendly Inns of North America.**

Ammenities
→ Handmade quilts, featherbeds
→ Porches with rocking chairs, blazing fireplaces, private baths
→ Library including books on local culture and history
→ Walking trails, birdwatching, gardens & wildflower walks
→ Peaceful environment with great views

Flexible Accommodations
→ Spacious farmhouse with rooms and suites
→ Restored 150 year old chestnut log cabin
→ Accommodation possibilities are many
  - *restful vacations & weekend getaways*
  - *romantic getaways*
  - *honeymoons*
  - *private dinners/celebrations*
  - *retreats*
  - *business meetings*
  - *corporate retreats*
  - *...and more*

Elegant Meals
→ Gourmet vegetarian meals: hearty breakfasts, lunches, and elegant dinners
→ Homemade pies, breads and pastas
→ Accommodations for dietary restrictions
→ Picnic lunches available

Convenient Central Kentucky Location
→ 20 minutes from I-75, 30 minutes from the Mountain Parkway
→ 75 minutes from Bluegrass International Airport in Lexington
→ Convenient to Kentucky's attractions, including
  - *Kentucky Horse Park*
  - *Renfro Valley Music Hall*
  - *Berea, Kentucky's Arts & Crafts Capital*
  - *Red River Gorge*
  - *Natural Bridge State Park*
  - *Lincoln's birthplace and boyhood home*
  - *Kentucky's Bourbon Trail*
  - *Mammoth Caves, Carter Caves*
  - *Horse farm tours by request*
  - *Horseback riding available nearby*
  - *Tater Knob and Bybee Potteries*

Contact Us
→ www.snughollow.com   → info@snughollow.com   →   (606) 723-4786